SPARK
PLUG

SPARK
PLUG

The Roadmap to Confidently Ignite and Navigate
Your Career Without Compromising Your Dreams

Nasrien E. Ibrahim, MD

**publish
your gift**

Published by Publish Your Gift®

An imprint of Purposely Created Publishing Group, LLC

Printed in the United States of America

ISBN: 978-1-64484-375-8 (print)
ISBN: 978-1-64484-376-5 (ebook)

Special discounts are available on bulk quantity purchases by book clubs, associations and special interest groups.
For details email: sales@publishyourgift.com or call (888) 949-6228.
For information log on to www.PublishYourGift.com

I dedicate this book to my mom, Salma, who is also a physician but did not get to practice medicine for very long because she chose to have four children and dedicate her life to raising the best family on this planet. Her love for my siblings and I is endless, and she makes us believe that there is nothing in this world we cannot accomplish. Thank you for never letting me quit. She is the epitome of unconditional love, strength, and sacrifice and a surrogate mom to so many.

To my dad, Ezzeldin, the man everyone says that I am his clone, who loves his family deeply, and who taught me the meaning of hard work and dedication to patients. He always tells my siblings and me to do good without expecting anything in return, and the universe will reward us for our good deeds. Thank you for always guiding me in my career and personal life. You always gives the best, most balanced advice and listen without judgment.

To my older sister, Rania, who truly is my biggest cheerleader. She has supported me during my highest and lowest moments and has loved me through some of my worst phases. I admire her personal growth and her dedication to living a truly peaceful life. She has shattered ceilings while remaining so humble, she does not know she is my hero. Thank you for letting my brothers and me tag along even when we were never as cool as you.

To my younger brother, Omar, who—although everyone thinks we are twins—is actually three years my junior. In many other ways, we are the exact same person. Thank you for rooting for me and for letting me share my deepest, darkest, and sometimes toughest secrets without judging me. Thank you for joining in on my crazy ideas and adventures and ending every serious conversation with belly laughter. He is the best cosmetic dermatologist on this planet and will keep me young forever. Thank you for flying in for every outrageous birthday party I throw, even if begrudgingly so.

To the baby of the Ibrahim family, Mostafa (a.k.a. Moose), the most cool, calm, and collected person I know. For being my voice of reason. For being the bravest person I know. He was the first person I told I planned to write a book, and he encouraged me to believe that I had something special to share with the world. He helped me organize the book, reminding me that I cannot have a career and money, without first having health, life, and human connections in order. I am forever grateful to him for heavily editing the first version of my book and providing incredibly thoughtful suggestions.

My family, all four MDs and two PhDs of us, means the world to me, and I love them from the deepest part of my soul. My siblings always say our family would have fallen apart without me, but little do they know, I would not be here (literally) without them. May God always protect them.

I dedicate my book to the souls that departed us way too soon—my four grandparents; my Uncle Mostafa who loved us like we were his own; my dad's brother Uncle Ali who loved my sister immensely; my mom's best friend Tunt Madiha who was a surrogate mom to me in Cincinnati and always reminded me that I am never alone because God is always with me; my mom's brother Uncle Ali who never wanted us to call him Uncle because he was forever young and never made my siblings and I feel out of place when we would visit Egypt in the summertime despite our mixed heritage and our broken Arabic; and my mom's sister Tunt Somaya who, despite having rheumatoid arthritis since her teen years, lived life to the absolute fullest: from us pushing her in her wheelchair at Disney World and cutting the lines to get on all the rides, to her infectious laugh, her love for everyone, for opening her home to anyone who needed a place to stay or a meal to eat, to sparking my love of makeup, to showing me what it meant to be classy and a badass, and to teaching your medical school students up until COVID-19 cruelly taking your life on December 1, 2020. Tunt Somaya, your memory lives on forever.

To the patients I have cared for, for the privilege of being a small part of their journey and teaching me more about life than they realize. For keeping me humble, for reminding me daily that the blood, sweat, and tears were worth it, and for sharing your magic with me on my toughest days.

I also dedicate this book to Dr. Lynelle Schneeberg, a pediatric sleep psychologist, who I met at the Harvard Writing, Publishing, and Social Media for Healthcare Professionals course in 2019. She was the first person to ever listen to my book pitch and comforted me when I broke down in tears while sharing some of the deepest stories of my life for the first time out loud. I met two other incredible women at that same course—Dr. Pascale Anglade and Dr. Sawsan Abdel-Raziq, a gastroenterologist and an internist, respectively, who I connected with immediately. (We have a WhatsApp group called

"The Badasses.") They sat with me at lunch to help perfect my book pitch and inspired me to put pen to paper.

To my business coach, Dr. Draion Burch, who saw something in me that I had not seen in myself, who has empowered me to live a purposeful life, and who has taught me to know my worth and demand it always. To my brand coach, Ms. Jai Stone, who brought my entire vision together, who inspired me to be my authentic self in everything I do, and who inspires me with her badassery on a regular basis. To Purposely Created Publishing Group™ for making my first book journey seamless.

To my mentors, sponsors, and coaches, whom I am forever indebted to for empowering me on my journey of personal and career growth and development. Thank you for believing in me, more than I believed in myself.

I dedicate this book to my friends and cousins, who I consider my sisters and brothers. I cannot name each one of you for the same reason I refuse to have bridesmaids—I have too many friends that I cherish and I cannot make one feel more important than the other. From the playgrounds in our compound in Al-Khobar, Saudi Arabia, my classmates in Manarat Al-Sharkia, my classmates at Indian Hill High School, my University of Cincinnati college, medical school, residency and fellowship friends, the friends I made in Cincinnati, Denver, and Boston, the sisters I hit the lottery with in Alpha Kappa Alpha, Sorority, Inc., my colleagues in medicine who became my family, and all the way to my teachers, professors, attendings, mentees, and trainees who have had an undeniable impact on my life. I have immense love for you.

And finally, to all the people along the way who told me my dreams were too unrealistic, or that I did not have "star quality" or who told me I was "too much." I thank you for igniting that fire within me to live life on my own terms.

SPARKPLUG IGNITER

noun

A person who creates an environment of inspired leadership and elevated growth.

SPARKPLUG FORMULA

FOREWORD

*Dr. Toniya Singh, Chair, Women in Cardiology Council
of the American College of Cardiology*

My name is Dr. Toniya Singh and, like Dr. Nasrien, I am an immigrant and a cardiologist. Also like her, I absolutely love people. Meeting them, talking to them, and learning from them. I also love reading, and I am so excited to introduce this absolutely fantastic book to you.

I knew of Dr. Nasrien through Twitter and then had the pleasure of meeting her in person at a cardiology conference in Paris. I was struck by her *joie de vivre*, her confidence, and the wonderful energy that surrounded her. Since then, I have gotten to know her better and have worked with her on various projects. She is a joy to work with. She leads with grace, shares the limelight willingly, and never loses an opportunity to make others shine.

Her story is told with authenticity and honesty. As Dr. Brené Brown stated, "Courage starts with showing up and letting ourselves be seen." By sharing her biggest challenges, Dr. Nasrien has shown up for herself and for us. Her focus on emotional and physical health is extremely important as it helps us stay strong for ourselves and our families. She also emphasizes the importance of setting boundaries and tapping into our passion to keep us excited, motivated, and happy.

Dr. Nasrien has struck a note that I know many physicians, scientists, and people building empires can relate to. We tend to be overachievers and perfectionists and indulge in practices that lead us to burnout. Many of us have trouble being our authentic selves as we feel that means we may not fit in. She encourages us to be ourselves. One of my favorite quotes is from Oscar Wilde that says, "Be yourself; everyone else is taken," and Dr. Nasrien stresses the importance of authenticity to living a content life.

I hope you enjoy this book as much as I did. Dr. Nasrien truly personifies the statement by Mahatma Gandhi to "Be the change you want to see in the world." I was elated with her successes, cast down by her failures, and knew she was someone I could relate to. As an action-oriented person, I particularly loved the questions at the end of every chapter that lead to reflection to help guide us forward. I am now firmly a member the army of Sparkies and hope to apply many of her valuable lessons to my life. I hope she ignites the same spark within you.

PREFACE

Hello and thank you for picking up my book! My name is Nasrien (pronounced NIS-REEN) Ezzeldin Ibrahim. I always include my middle initial E. because Ezzeldin is my dad's name, and he has played an immeasurable role in my life; he also gave me my nickname since birth—Neeno (actually Neeno Beeno)—and most of my close friends and family call me Neeno.

I was born in Al-Khobar, Saudi Arabia, to my Egyptian mom, Salma, and my Sudanese dad, Ezzeldin, and grew up around other expatriates in a compound until the age of 15. My parents wanted my siblings and I to have the best educational opportunities, so they applied for immigration to the United States. We were Sudanese kids. (You do not get Saudi citizenship when you are born there unless your father is a Saudi citizen.) Growing up in an expatriate world, our opportunities were never going to be equivalent to those Saudi citizens had. We were granted approval and immigrated to the United States; Cincinnati, Ohio to be exact. Why Ohio you ask? Because my parents had friends there. My dad could not immigrate with us because he is a physician and would have to start all over to be able to practice in the United States. Leaving my dad was the first time I got my heart broken. My siblings, mom, and I found our way, and soon enough, Cincinnati, Ohio, became home. The move was rough to put it lightly, but eventually I was able to take every bit of me that belonged to all those countries and become the woman I am today—a Sudanese Egyptian American immigrant woman who realized the American Dream.

I completed high school in Cincinnati and then stayed for college, medical school, my residency, and my general cardiology fellowship. It took a long time for Cincinnati to become home, so I was so afraid of leaving and starting over again someplace new. Then I did. I moved to Denver for my second fellowship, which was in advanced heart failure and transplant cardiology. Denver was really where I grew up. I did not know a soul when I arrived. I had to start from scratch—make new friends, find a gym, find a grocery store, and get comfortable in my new home. My fellowship was incredible, the city and people were incredible, and you cannot beat 300 days of sunshine. Denver is where I became my most confident, independent, adult self. I experienced a lot of internal growth. After Denver, I moved to Boston for my third fellowship, which was in clinical cardiology research, much to the chagrin of my older sister who jokingly asked how many more graduations she had to attend. Four years of college, four years of medical school, three years of residency, and six years of fellowship later I finally got my "real" job as an attending physician and researcher in the field of advanced heart failure and transplant cardiology.

The American Dream, right? Well, it was not all rainbows and sunshine like I thought it was supposed to be. My journey has had wins and losses, which I learned to appreciate as lessons. My move to Boston was rough. I left a toxic relationship. I was training in an institution that I did not feel I belonged in/deserved to be at (more on imposter syndrome later), I was in a super expensive and cold (the weather and the people) city with short summers, and I felt totally out of place. It created the perfect storm for the lowest point in my career where I was depressed and, for the first time ever, thought about suicide. I had to save myself and I did. I am beyond grateful I am here to share my story and beyond grateful you are taking the time to read it. The road to the American Dream is full of grit and perseverance.

My lowest point taught me so much. It was the blessing in disguise I needed to really live my fullest life. My well-being became a focus of my life. It always was important to me; I always spoke about the importance of having a life outside of medicine and academia, but my lowest point took the importance of wellness to a whole other level. I have incorporated practices into my life that have helped me succeed as a person, a physician, a researcher, and an academician. I have blogged, given talks, been interviewed on podcasts, and tweeted about my journey and the lessons I have learned, but I wanted a platform with no character limit to share my blueprint to confidently navigating your career without compromising your life dreams and navigating your life without compromising your career dreams. My book is a memoir, interwoven with advice that you can apply to the growth and development of your own career and life. In other words, I am going to teach you how to be a badass both at work and in your life outside of it.

Get ready to turn your SPARK on.

Everything will change. The only question is growing up or decaying.

—Nikki Giovanni

INTRODUCTION

Before you read any further, I want you to put this book down and write a letter to yourself. Write about everything you have accomplished at school, in life, and in your career. Write about everything you love about yourself. Write about the people whose lives you touched. Write about the friends and family you love. Write about the things that make you happy. Write about the impact you have had in this world. The letter can be as long or as short as you want it to be, but I want you to write about all the amazing things you have done. Keep it on your nightstand, we will get back to this letter later.

After you have written your letter, grab your favorite bookmark and highlighter and prepare to be ignited.

CHAPTER 1

HEALTH SPARK

EMOTIONAL HEALTH

We begin with emotional health because of how important it is to the growth and development of every other part of ourselves. I can now reflect on big life events that I was depressed during. Certainly, the move from Saudi Arabia to the United States was rough on me, my siblings, and our mom. I was taken away from the friends who I considered sisters and brothers who I had known since early childhood—some literally since birth—and my first "boyfriend." I was catapulted into an entirely new world. As an adult, I know my parents sacrificed more than I could ever appreciate so we could have the best chance at an education and life, but in that moment, I hated them for making us come to the United States. Everything from the way the toothpaste tasted to the lack of diversity in the high school I attended was foreign. I failed my first exam ever in life (American History) because I did not study. I remember going to a party in high school and not telling my mom where I was and her losing her shit on me when I got home at 2 in the morning because she could not get a hold of me. I was acting out to punish them. I still feel guilty about that. She was stressed too—she was essentially a single mother in a country completely foreign to her. It was the first time I can recall being depressed. I did not tell anyone or talk about it. I sort of just shuffled through it.

I finally became happy when I started college. I had the time of my life. There were finally people who looked like me from many different walks of life. I felt like I belonged. Medical school and training were incredible experiences, and each had their ups and downs. Although the work was tiring and the hours were long, I was in awe of my peers. I was no longer the smartest person in class—everyone was smart and competitive. It was also the first time I confronted death and illness head on. My dad is an oncologist, so I heard stories he told my mom about young patients with stage IV breast cancer, but now I was the physician, and that level of sadness and disappointment was more personal. These were difficult, but they were not the huge periods of depression I would later experience in Boston.

I was ecstatic about the opportunity to train at an Ivy League institution, but I was unprepared for the rough transition. It was my first experience with imposter syndrome, and I had left sunny Denver to move to a gloomy, cold city. I consider myself a Midwestern gal, and it was culture shock when I moved to Boston—warm smiles, friendly good mornings from passersbys, and small talk at the coffee shop were replaced with horns honking and cyclists getting cussed at by drivers. It was nuts. On top of that, the move to Boston was the catalyst to my leaving a toxic relationship. My rent for a ground floor one-bedroom apartment was outrageous, and I had to figure out how to survive on a fellow salary in one of the most expensive cities in the United States. And ooh wee, when winter came, and the sunset was at 4:30 p.m., I thought my usual "winter blues" had come on. (I am a summer baby; the beach is my favorite place on earth.) Instead of winter blues, I went into a deep depression.

This was the kind of depression where you question every decision you have made in life that brought you to the place you are. Depression where you must force yourself to get out of bed. Depression where you eat and drink to numb your pain. Depression where you go to bootcamp twice a day because the endorphins make you feel good temporarily. Depression where you are sitting in your bathtub crying for your parents. Depression like you have never experienced before. Depression like the whole world is closing in on you. Depression like you feel like a big black cloud will not leave from above you. I hope you have not experienced this, but if you have, you know just how bad it can get.

I knew exactly what it was, but I did not have the courage to get help. I researched my institution's employee assistance program and the services it provided, but I did not feel brave enough to give them a call. I knew if someone diagnosed me with depression, I would have to include it as a "disability" in medical licensing forms of some states. My siblings always told me that I was the strongest among them and that without me, our family would have fallen apart a long time ago. I could not admit to them that I was suffering. I knew I could find support within my family and friends, but I never wanted anyone to worry about me—especially not my parents who lived thousands of miles away. I suffered in silence and drenched my pillow with desperate tears on more nights than I care to recall. It was a dark time.

One winter morning I was walking to work, and I stood on an island in the middle of a busy intersection. I saw a huge truck coming down the street. I thought, *What if I just step out into traffic and let this truck hit me? Only then, would I not be in so much pain.* I did not, mainly because I knew my death would destroy my family. So when I say they are the reason I am still here, it is not because my parents created me, it is because they saved me that day without even realizing it. That was the moment I knew I had to save myself. I went to employee assistance that same day and received a referral to a psychiatrist to start treatment for depression. I broke down so bad at my first appointment that I remember the psychiatrist bringing her attending in (the psychiatrist was a resident). The attending psychiatrist asked me if anyone was abusing me at work. It took several months for me to feel like myself again, for me to feel like that huge black cloud was lifted from above me, for me to remember all the goals I was planning to crush, for me to feel happy again, and for me to remember how much I loved life.

My outlook on life changed forever. I still take my medication, and I still go to therapy once a month. In fact, I think everyone should see a therapist. We would all benefit from speaking to someone regularly who does not know us and has no vested interest in our lives. Our family and friends can support us, but having a shoulder to lean on or someone to vent to is not the same as speaking to a professional trained to help you. As with every relationship, you must find a therapist you connect with; sessions will not be valuable if you are unable to spill your heart out. Many successful individuals have mood disorders that go undiagnosed or untreated because of shame or fear of appearing to be "weak"—a concept I find ludicrous. Those of us in medicine face death on a regular basis. Those of us who are researchers are under an immense amount of stress—grant funding, promotions, office politics, imposter syndrome, among other stressors. And, of course, these are not the only professions that experience this. Burnout affects everyone. It leads to anxiety, depression, and other mood disorders. Part of a healthy mind is the mindset. We can change the way we think about things by replacing negative, self-deprecating thoughts with positive, empowering ones. This takes work, but the reward is priceless.

Take time to heal your mind. Without a healed mind, everything else becomes challenging. A healed mind can accomplish so much more, but also, a healed mind puts you in a position where hardly anything phases you. The world around us is extremely chaotic, so we must take the time to heal internally before taking on the external. We should all place an emphasis on mental and emotional health like we do physical health. With a healthy mind you become indestructible and everything else falls into place. My advice to you: find a therapist you connect with and meet with them on a regular basis. Take time each day to nurture your mental well-being—whether by meditation, outdoor walks, journaling, listening to music, or whatever it is that puts your mind at ease. And please, do not worry about what others may think of you—even if "others" are a state medical licensing board. (We seriously need to get rid of that ridiculous clause.)

We all have trauma that we have to work through, but I have learned that you only truly live life when your emotional health is healed. I started evaluating my emotional wellness like I did my physical wellness. Therapy taught me to deal with circumstances more ably and to count losses as lessons. To change my mindset. To be optimistic. That everyone has a story behind them. That I needed routines and exercise was key to my overall wellness. That I had to learn how to forgive and let go and not take things so personally. That I had to stop letting mundane things trigger me. That I had to work on my patience and harbor less anger and resentment. I realized that while I thought I was in a good place, Boston showed me I was not where I needed to be. That I had to resolve the bad relationships and life experiences that I never really processed. That all the material things and the parties and clubs were escapes from my insecurities, and so I had to really dig deep down and heal my mind. The things on this list are my realizations, and you will come to your own as you begin to heal your mind. Even if you cannot afford therapy— because I do realize it can be outrageously priced—engage in other activities that help heal your mind. Some options are meditation, hobbies that help us express our inner struggles such as music and art, and reading or writing poetry.

Life will always hand us blows when we least expect it, but when your mind is healed, the blows do not strike as hard. What worked for me may not work for everyone, so we each must find our own therapy. I have found being open with friends, trainees, colleagues, and patients alike about my depression and how treatment literally saved my life has encouraged them to act to transform their own lives. In sharing your pain, you help others heal. I knew I could not live much longer under than big black cloud and I do not want you to have to either. Reach out. Get help. Speak up. You may save a life.

SPARK Suggestions

1. Make an appointment with a therapist. You can even meet them virtually from the comfort of your home. Not everyone needs medications, but everyone can stand to benefit from speaking with a therapist. We all have challenges in our lives we have had to and will continue to need to overcome.

2. If someone around you does not seem like their normal self, reach out. Not just in a "hey, how are you" way, but in a "how are you REALLY doing way." You could be the catalyst to them seeking help. No one should suffer in silence.

3. Make a mental well-being exercise part of your daily routine. I personally meditate for ten minutes and journal for five minutes every single morning. I find both practices help to remove thoughts from my head and put them onto a piece of paper, allowing me to start my day fresh.

4. Love yourself deeply.

SPARK Notes

PHYSICAL HEALTH

Why is physical health critically important? Oh, for so many reasons—and looking good is last on my list. Of course, since I am a cardiologist, I must tell you that exercise is important for your heart and to live a long and healthy life. But let me be the first to tell you, I hated exercising for the longest time. I begrudgingly dragged my butt to the gym because I wanted to look good and I also did not want to be a fraud. I am telling patients to exercise daily and here I am, the only exercise I like is dancing to trap music at the club? Not acceptable. So, I had to find an exercise regimen that was fun, and I had to change my mindset.

Let us take a step back first, and then I will get back to telling you how amazing exercising is. Routine primary care checkups are mandatory! I am looking at you my fellow physicians—we are the worst! And I am looking at you too—people of cultural backgrounds who do not feel strongly about prevention and routine primary care visits. This includes where my roots originate. We must break this cycle. Let me tell you why: Sometimes a disease such as hypertension or diabetes can be brewing for a long time and we may have no symptoms at all until it is too late and the damage to multiple organs has occurred including the heart, liver, and kidneys. Routine checkups, while sometimes anxiety-provoking, are critical. (I personally dislike going to see my primary care clinician because I am always paranoid that she is going to find something wrong with me.) Your primary care clinician examines you and checks appropriate laboratory tests to monitor you for diseases and to guide you on preventative measures—routine colonoscopies, mammograms, pap smears, and so forth. And just as important is routine eye exams and dental checkups. Why? Because we cannot always tell when something is wrong, and it is better to find out early than when it may be too late. I remember meeting a young patient who had not seen a clinician in several years and was found to have asymptomatic hypertension that resulted in end-stage kidney disease requiring transplant—something that likely was preventable.

Besides, we need to be in the best mental and physical health for everything else to fall into place. I also think it is important to show our parents and the generations before us the importance of routine preventative healthcare and to be role models for the generations coming after us. Make yearly appointments with your primary care clinician, your dentist, and your eye doctor and bring all your family members and friends with you! Not literally, but you get my point. Let us be the generation that changes the burden of disease in our Black and brown communities.

So back to exercise: it is free therapy! I was self-medicating in my deepest state of depression by going to bootcamp twice a day because the endorphins felt so good but only lasted temporarily. Clearly not a fix. It is no substitute for therapy but in my opinion, it goes hand in hand with mental well-being. There are published guidelines regarding how much exercise you should partake in per week, but I say just start somewhere. I tell patients all the time start with five minutes a day, then increase what you are doing to thirty minutes a day. I personally find that I enjoy group classes the most, and I love classes with a tough but kind instructor who plays great music. I am not one to go into a gym and try to figure out what to do with the weights or equipment, I prefer an instructor telling me what to do and to be on me when I am fooling around in class. I also find that exercising with a friend always means I am more likely to show up to class—the no-show fines do not bother me enough.

For me, exercising in the morning is a great way to start each day, and keeps me from finding excuses not to exercise later in the day—especially on those winter nights when your couch and a cup of hot chocolate sound much more tempting. I love having my evenings completely free to meet up for happy hour, work on a paper, or just relax with my reality TV shows. But again, just find something you love that makes your heart rate go up that you can do for thirty minutes each day. Think about that—that is half of an episode of Real Housewives of Atlanta. (One of my guilty pleasures!) And your routine does not have to be fancy or expensive. I love classes, but it is cheap (or free) to get out and walk or run, try a virtual class online, or go swimming. Exercise to protect your heart and encourage your family members and friends to join in. Find accountability partners, and you will be more likely to stick with it.

Lastly, when you exercise you feel good and you look good. It is just you and the treadmill or bike. Your mind is clear, and you are filled with a rush of endorphins. Make exercise part of your daily routine just like brushing your teeth is. And do not beat yourself up about missing a few days here and there, but because it is harder to get back on track, do anything you can to get back in a good routine. Routine exercise builds confidence. Your future self will thank you for it. So will your wallet! (Healthier individuals pay less in medical costs.) What is not to love about free therapy, confidence, looking good, and cost savings?

So, go on out and find a fabulous workout plan for you and your friends and make sure you are scheduled for your annual checkup with your primary care clinician. Prevention is the best medicine.

 **SPARK Suggestions**

1. See your primary care clinician on an annual basis, at least. Make sure you are scheduled for routine preventative health measures including colonoscopies, dental cleanings, and pap smears.

2. Find an activity you like to do that brings your heart rate up and you can do for at least thirty minutes a day, and make it part of your daily routine.

3. Encourage your family members and friends to seek routine preventative care and to exercise regularly. We only get better when we change the communities around us.

4. Love yourself deeply.

SPARK Notes

SPIRITUAL HEALTH

Let me be clear: I do not mean religion here. Religion is something extremely private that I do not engage in conversations about. I do believe all religions at their core have similar teachings of that we should be good human beings and we should love everyone. That message is lost I think, and religion has been used to divide people, cause wars, and break up families. I also do not agree with everything taught in major religions. For example, that gay people are sinners and will burn in hell. I cannot and will never agree with that teaching. So, I do not discuss religion because I feel strongly that it is something so private and my message to everyone on earth, regardless of what religion you follow or do not follow, is to simply be a good person and treat everyone well. So, what about spirituality?

Spirituality to me is the connection with something bigger than oneself and realizing that "that something bigger than yourself" is also found within yourself. It is the purity of the soul. It is the realization of the connection of our inner soul with everything and everyone. It is disconnecting from all the worldly things that are fleeting yet occupy so much of our mind and energy. It is the ability to empathize with those around us and the ability to connect on a deeper level. The most spiritual people I know are the kindest, purest, most humble souls. Their positive energy emanates when you are in their presence. They have an enormous amount of love within them and they never hold back sharing that love with the world. I love being around them because being around them forces me to look at the world in a kinder, gentler way.

And why is spirituality important? Because when you have healed your emotional and physical health, a healed soul brings you the type of contentment we all dream of. You become truly unbreakable. The goal is for your soul to align with your personality and mental well-being. When they are in synch, everything in life works seamlessly. When you are too tied up with the fleeting world (mental/personality/ego), you are in constant conflict with the pureness and love of the soul, and that causes stress.

Let me tell you about my experience with meditation. When my leadership coach, Mr. Jim McKenna, suggested I try meditation, I laughed. I was thinking, is this man crazy? Do I look like someone who goes on those silent retreats in the mountains for days? No way. Well, I agreed to try meditation because everything he has ever coached me to do has been extremely useful to my personal development. I agreed to start with five minutes a day... only! That was the maximum amount of time I was willing to give this silly exercise. I decided I was going to get to my office early and meditate there. On day one of meditation, I remember turning on my computer and being annoyed that those five minutes I "had" to meditate for could be better spent checking my email. Then I realized how crazy I sounded, that I would rather delete unnecessary emails for five minutes than do something that was healthy for my mind and well-being. I turned my computer off, locked my office door, put my headphones on, and I was hooked forever.

I began with five-minute meditations and today I meditate every morning. I have made meditation part of my daily routine. After my first week of meditating daily (which is the maximum amount of time I told my leadership coach I was willing to try), I slept better than I had ever slept in my life. I felt so well-rested and I specifically recall how much better my attitude was during early morning work meetings. One day I looked around the room and asked myself, why is everyone so mad? Then I texted my friends who were in the same meeting jokingly that we should start each meeting with a meditation. Prayer is a form of meditation too. In Islam, we pray five times a day (I must admit I do not always do this), and that is five opportunities to meditate. Listening to the Quran in beautiful recitations is also soothing to my soul and a form of meditation. I recommend meditation to my friends and patients who look at me the same way I looked at my leadership coach, but I have never received negative feedback on this recommendation!

Like exercise, I recommend meditating in the morning, particularly those of us who work in high-stress careers. It is a way to completely disconnect, to rest and recharge your mind, and to heal your soul. I also meditate before an event or situation that makes me super anxious. It always helps. If you want to try meditation, find an app for beginners or a YouTube Video or Spotify playlist—make sure you like the meditation teacher's voice, so you do not feel annoyed—and give it a try. To really get a sense of how it may benefit your life, I recommend trying it for a week straight before giving up on it. Even beginning with five minutes a day like I did will make a difference in your soul's well-being. So yes, I did apologize to my leadership coaching for thinking he was crazy to recommend meditating to me. It was one of the best suggestions he has given for my overall well-being. For that, I am thankful.

We will discuss gratitude in a bit more detail later, but I believe gratitude is tied to spirituality. Gratitude for things you have and gratitude for things yet to come increases your spiritual capital. When life feels completely out of control, staying grateful makes it easier to deal with. The more grateful you are, the more abundant your life is, even when nothing material changes. My little brother Moose taught me this.

Find whatever it is that helps you disconnect from the world and make it part of your daily routine. Whether it is prayer or meditation or any form of activity that allows you to separate yourself from all the worries of the world. If you do not know where to start, start with meditation. Put your headphones in and prepare to clear your mind. I mean really clear the clutter. Give it a try! You will sleep like a baby.

⚡ SPARK Suggestions

1. Only discuss religion with people who are open to the conversation. To some people, religion is an extremely private thing and there are some who neither believe in God nor religion. Read the room.

2. Find a beginner's meditation app and give it a try. Meditate consistently for a week before giving up on it.

3. When you notice an improvement in your sleep and attitude, recommend meditation to your family members, friends, colleagues, and trainees. My best friend once told me that all super successful people meditate. I do not know how true that is, but I believe him.

4. Love yourself deeply.

SPARK Notes

_____

_____

_____

_____

_____

_____

_____

_____

_____

_____

_____

_____

_____

_____

_____

_____

_____

_____

_____

_____

_____

_____

_____

_____

_____

_____

_____

_____

_____

_____

SELF-LOVE

It took me until I was an adult to really love myself. I was a Sudanese-Egyptian girl growing up as an expatriate in Saudi Arabia. I never felt like Sudan was home, while my dad is from there, I have never been there. I never considered Egypt home, my mom's whole family is there, and we spent summers there, but it never felt like home. And we lived in Saudi Arabia as expatriates or foreigners. That was not home either. I did have an amazing childhood in Saudi Arabia growing up in a compound with friends whom I now consider family. We were blissfully oblivious to the world outside of our compound. All of us "Third Culture Kids" are spread all over the world but keep in touch, we share similar childhoods that make it easy for us to relate to each other even as adults.

I did not feel like I belonged to any country until I came to the United States. I feel incredibly lucky my parents brought us here, even though I hated them for it at the age of fifteen when I was torn away from everything I was accustomed to and loved. The United States took us in and allowed us to be who we were and live out our childhood dreams. I always knew I wanted to become a physician because both of my parents are physicians, but I never in a million years dreamed I would be taking care of patients at world-class institutions, publishing papers, and giving talks all over the world. I am forever grateful this country took my family and me in and finally gave us a place to call home.

It was this sense of finally belonging somewhere that sparked my journey to self-love. Imposter syndrome, which we will discuss in more detail in a later chapter, can be a consequence of low self-love, low self-worth, and low self-confidence. Now when I look back, I recognize that it crept into my life on a regular basis. I hated my curly hair when I was young, I always wanted my mom to straighten it for me because that is what I thought beauty was. I always felt like I was too dark. I remember one summer in Egypt when I was a little girl someone said to me that I needed to stay out of the sun because no one would want to marry me because I was too dark. I remember my Sudanese friends and I being called slaves in our compound. Like most countries, fair skin, light eyes, and straight hair were the standards of beauty. Or maybe it was because every time we landed in the Cairo airport with our Sudanese passports as children, we were always held at immigrations for hours, my poor mom with three kids going through hours of questioning, explaining to the immigration officers that although my baby brother had a name in common with a terrorist, we were in fact, not terrorists.

When we immigrated to the United States, I went to a predominantly white school, so I still did not feel like I belonged. I only started to feel like I belonged when I went to college and saw people from all racial and ethnic backgrounds from all walks of life. I am ashamed to admit that for the longest time I denied my Sudanese half because that was the "Black" side. I embraced my Black side when I went to college. That is where my journey to self-love began. I saw people around me that looked just like me, living authentically and unapologetically. I fell in love with the Black half, the Sudanese half, and proudly spoke of my Sudanese-Egyptian background. I embraced my complex background, my curly hair, and the color of my skin, especially when I got several shades darker in the summertime! I wish people realized that things said to children can continue to hurt us as adults.

When we acknowledge that we are perfectly imperfect, self-love will ensue. I remember words from my wellness coach, Dr. Darshan Mehta, that I will forever repeat to myself: "Perfection is a sick mindset." We must be kind to ourselves. I know many successful people that are hard on themselves, but we all must remember to be kind and gentle to ourselves. Think about how you treat your best friend in the whole wide world. You would never want to hurt them, right? So that is how you should treat yourself. If we cannot love ourselves to the depths of the ocean, then how can we expect others to love us. Find the pieces of you that you find the hardest to love, ask yourself why, and then love them deeply. Wake up each day and look at yourself in the mirror and realize how beautiful your soul is. And I do not want you to just say you love yourself, really work on it. None of us are perfect, but we are all special, and that love we give others, we deserve that too.

One day when you are ready, look at yourself in the mirror completely naked. See what parts of your physical body you want to learn to love and what parts of your soul that you can see through your eyes that you also want to learn to love, then begin your journey to self-acceptance and self-love. The same love you are giving others needs to be poured into your own soul. It is only when we can love ourselves deeply that we are able to genuinely and fully receive love from others.

Change the narrative that runs through your mind. We are our own worst critics, and we are extraordinarily hard on ourselves. When negative thoughts come into your mind, replace them with positive ones. Kind and loving ones. The same kind of love you would shower your best friend with, turn that light towards your soul. What naturally follows a health mind and body, is a healthy soul. Love yourself, every piece of yourself, to the depths of your soul.

SPARK Suggestions

1. Be kind to yourself. Always.

2. Remember as my wellness coach said: "Perfection is a sick mindset."

3. Find the things you dislike about yourself, and work on loving those deeply. We must love ourselves for others to love us just as deeply.

4. Love yourself deeply.

SPARK Notes

_____

_____

_____

_____

_____

_____

_____

_____

_____

_____

_____

_____

_____

_____

_____

_____

_____

_____

_____

_____

_____

_____

_____

_____

CHAPTER 2

LIFE SPARK

SOUL SPARK

I remember seeing this quote circulating on Instagram: "Be fearless in the pursuit of that which sets your soul on fire." It resonated with me profoundly. When we figure out what sparks joy in our souls, we need to incorporate that into our careers and lives. I cannot imagine life passing me by without doing the things I love doing—money-making or not. Imagine getting paid for doing something you are passionate about? I think that is what people mean when they describe their "dream job."

I believe we all have a purpose here on earth. When you think of all the things you love doing and would do for free, those are the things you are passionate about. When you think of all the things people tell you that you are good at, those are your gifts. And we all have a gift. My business coach, Dr. Draion Burch, teaches that combining your passions and your gifts defines your purpose. There is no better way to live life than with purpose. That is how you live fully. Your passion is something you are good at, something you love doing, and something that can make you money, and something that you can continuously grow and learn in.

And just to be clear, our purpose does not necessarily have to be the careers we are in, although that would be amazing.

Teachers for example, are changing the world by educating and empowering our next generation, and that may be someone's purpose on this earth. I for example, cannot imagine myself being anything other than a physician, and if I had to, I would do this for free. It is my passion. I also love mentoring people, especially underrepresented minorities, along their journeys in medicine. I do this for free, not because I must, but because seeing my mentees succeed sets my soul on fire. As does the opportunity to play a role, even if small, in changing the face of medicine.

We must remember that every career is needed, every career is valuable, and every career is important for the world as we know it to function. The world cannot function without each one of us—teachers, lawyers, physicians, artists, plumbers, chefs, farmers, sanitation workers, and musicians, and more. Every career has an impact on the world around us. Maybe you are in your career only to pay your bills and that is okay too. We all need to be financially secure, but I implore you to not give up on the dreams the child inside you has always had. Find a way to either incorporate that into your career—for me it is coaching and motivational speaking—or make time weekly or monthly to incorporate it into your life. Do not let those dreams die. The dreams that give purpose to our lives. The dreams that keep you young at heart and keep that fire in your soul lit.

At the end of our lives, the number of papers we published, the number of cases we crushed, or the number of awards we won do not matter. What matters is that we lived a life of purpose, we left a legacy behind, we changed the communities and lives around us, we empowered others to live out their dreams too, we lived fully, and we truly loved our lives. So, forget what society or your family expect you to do. They are not the ones living your life. You are. You have nothing to prove to anyone but yourself. Find whatever it is that sparks joy in your soul and make it part of your life. We all deserve to live a life of purpose that we truly love.

How would it feel to go to sleep on Sunday nights without the "Sunday Scaries" but excited to wake up on Monday morning? That is the type of life you want to build for yourself. By living life on your own terms while fulfilling your purpose, you empower those around you to do the same. And what a world that would be? Where everyone is living out their true purpose. I know it would be a happy and content world.

And sometimes when I talk about finding a career that aligns with your purpose, people think I am only speaking of physicians, firefighters, paramedics, etc.… who save people on a daily basis—but this is far from the truth. Musicians heal the world with their music; music is therapy. Artists heal the world with their art; art is therapy. Teachers empower the next generation through education and through healing the minds and souls of students all over the world. Plumbers make our lives easier, grocery store workers are essential to our existence, and chefs heal our bodies. Passions can be ignited by service to others. And every career has some type of service. That is the best way to live a life of purpose. A purposeful life is one that fulfills your needs, while at the same time helping others. It is doing something bigger than yourself. Every single person has a unique purpose; it may take time to figure out what your purpose is, but when you do, it will be as though a light has been ignited in your soul.

Live fully. Live with purpose. Love the life you are living. The late great Dr. Maya Angelou said, "Your legacy is every life you touched." So touch as many as you can while here on earth and your presence will be felt long after you are gone.

SPARK Suggestions

1. Write down the things you dreamed of doing as a child and find a way to incorporate those into your career. If not in your career, then in the life you have outside of your career.

2. Write down everything you would do even if you were not getting paid to do it (passions) and write down everything people tell you that you are good at (gifts).

3. Like my business coach, Dr. Draion Burch, teaches, find a way to combine your passions and gifts to identify your purpose. Then live in your purpose.

4. Love yourself deeply.

SPARK Notes

AUTHENTICITY

It is extremely stressful to always put on a front, whether at work, around friends, or around family. No matter what you feel you must hide or change because of fear of not being accepted, it is distressing to not live your life as you wish to in all arenas. Hiding who you are becomes tiring. It is tricky in certain fields, industries, and workplaces that have traditions and customs that might be old school—the "this is how we have always done it" kind of thinking. The expectation to conform can be distressing.

The first time I ever went on an interview was for medical school. I was so nervous, and I wanted to make sure I was accepted, so I asked people I trusted and who were in positions of leadership within medical school what I should wear, how I should style my hair, and what to expect. When I was in college, college advisors advised me to pretend that everyone interviewing me was an old, white, conservative man who wears a bowtie on a regular basis. The advice felt weird, but I wanted to get into medical school so, I complied. I dressed accordingly—conservative colored skirt suits, hair straightened, pale colored nails, minimal makeup, pearl earrings. I answered questions asked of me in a way that would not offend an old, white, conservative man who wears a bow tie.

Let me tell you, this was the worst advice ever given to me, and I carried it along my journey in medicine. I ended up doing one residency and three fellowships, and I had to interview for each of those and every single time I thought of that terrible advice. "Old white conservative man." Meanwhile, interviewers were asking me things like what my plans for having a family were, whether I was single and did not mind giving my cell phone number out so "We can connect at the next cardiology conference, but do not tell anyone I asked for your number," and whether I was sure I wanted to do cardiology because it is a tough field and I may not have enough time for a family.

It was not until I got my first "real" job out of training that I realized how foolish the advice I had been following was. Now, I dare anyone to ask me any of those inappropriate questions or make any of those ridiculous statements. I started wearing my hair curly as a protest to what a physician is supposed to look like, and I began wearing pink blazers and dresses on stage. I also spoke about all the things I love doing outside of work and discovered how many people think that physicians do not have normal lives outside of medicine! I love college basketball, LeBron James, trap music, going to concerts, day parties, beach trips, and getting glammed up for galas. I spoke about taboo things like depression, dissatisfaction at work, and burnout. I stopped caring about what people thought I was supposed to look like, speak like, or act like. In being myself, I could connect with patients better, and my colleagues and trainees seemed to appreciate me for it.

I remember my work friends asking me how I connected with a seemingly reserved and serious older colleague of ours, and I said, "Oh, we talked about the Alabama/Louisiana State University football game, and we became friends after that." Be your authentic self; it is so much easier than trying to be someone you think the people around you expect you to be. To be completely honest, I am not always sure how to advise my mentees in how they should wear their hair or dress for interviews in this conservative world of medicine. I never want to be the reason they do not get selected for a position, but I do ask them if they really want to be at an institution that does not embrace them just the way they are? I would not.

So, go on, be your badass self. Live life on your own terms. If you are doing excellent work and being kind to everyone around you, you will be respected and appreciated. We do our best work when we do not feel as though we must put on a show or live life to fit someone else's expectations. I know I became much happier, confident, and courageous when I started showing up to everything I did as my true self. You cannot expect everyone to love you, but make sure the institution you work for accepts you just the way you are. They are lucky to have you. And without even realizing it, living authentically encourages everyone around you to do the same.

Living an inauthentic life is exhausting. It is as though you are auditioning for a different role every hour of the day. Living authentically allows you to connect with people with similar interests and opinions as you, and it encourages others to express themselves freely as well. Whether you are an administrative assistant or an executive, bring the parts of you that make you special to the work you are doing. You were given the position for a reason, so come as your authentic self, your whole self; it is much less exhausting, and that allows you to expend your energy in other avenues that contribute to your career development. Be courageous and confident enough to live authentically and to show up in everything you do as your true self.

I am granting you permission to live authentically. Always.

SPARK Suggestions

1. Do excellent work.

2. Be kind to others.

3. Live authentically.

4. Love yourself deeply.

SPARK Notes

CONFIDENCE AND COURAGE

Confidence comes when your mind, body, and soul are healed. Confidence comes when you are doing something you love. Confidence comes when you are living life on your own terms. Confidence comes when you are living authentically. Confidence comes when you realize that no one is perfect. Confidence comes when you realize everyone struggles with something that is not always apparent to the rest of the world. Confidence comes when you find and are living your true purpose.

Confidence can be gained and lost, and it is something we must continuously develop. We always hear about women struggling with confidence more than men. I have been told to "Have the confidence of a mediocre white man" more times than I can count. It is something that I have had to work on in my career. My confidence in my regular life was never something I struggled with but when imposter syndrome creeped in, being outside of my comfort zone and being immersed in a whole new world in medicine—the research world—I realized I was not as confident as I would like to be.

But confidence in your abilities is easier to build when your mind, body, and soul are healthy. Remember I said, when all three of those are healthy, you become unbreakable? Confidence can be lost too. When you fail an exam or lose a big case, it is easy to feel discouraged. But if we have a healthy mind, body, and soul, the time to recover from those hits becomes shorter and shorter. Confidence is learning that success does not come without failures and roadblocks and the understanding that everyone's path to success varies and is seldom a straight line. Confidence comes when you stop worrying about what everyone around you thinks, because most of the time, others are not even thinking about you. They are too worried what others may think of them. Confidence comes when we become kind to ourselves, when we love ourselves, when we learn to roll with the punches, and when we realize every loss is a blessing in disguise as long as we recognize the lessons in the losses.

Confidence is the realization that you have something to share with the world and you share it without reservation. I used to hate public speaking. I would have so much anxiety the evening before I had to give a talk, and the day of the talk, my heart would be racing. I never even remembered all that I spoke about because I was extremely nervous. The shocking thing to me was people told me they could barely tell how nervous I was. Meanwhile, I felt like I was dying inside every time I stood on stage. I remember once asking my primary care physician to prescribe a beta blocker (a medication that slows down your heart rate and can reduce your stage fright) for me to take before I had to give a talk. I was exceptionally nervous for a talk once, I took two tablets instead of the prescribed single tablet and, oh my, was that a terrible idea. My blood pressure plummeted, and I was in the restroom throwing up minutes before I had to give my talk. My brother Omar and I laughed about it after the fact, but that was the last time I took the medicine. In fact, the pill bottle is still sitting in my medicine cabinet.

I read books on public speaking and watched YouTube videos for tips, and they all shared a common theme: keep doing it, and it will get easier. You do not have to feel confident every time, just keep acting confident. When you keep acting confident, you will start feeling it. That is what I did. I started speaking up more at smaller meetings and accepted every invitation big or small to give a talk. I found it much easier to speak on topics I was passionate about. And preparation was key to diffusing my anxiety. My mentor, Dr. Jim Januzzi, always said to me that the audience wants you to succeed. I also found that being my authentic self on stage helps me feel more confident and allows me to connect with the audience better. If you want to increase your confidence, speak up every opportunity you get—and disregard the worry about what others will think. (Remember, they are not thinking about you anyway.) Sit at the table—at the head of it if you are leading the meeting or as close to it as possible if not. And be present in every meeting, give your opinion fearlessly, be prepared by practicing out loud, talk about things you are passionate about, and bring your authentic self to every encounter you have. The world wants to experience the real you.

With confidence comes courage. The courage to speak up and to show up as your authentic self. The bravest thing I did was share the lowest point in my career—my deep depression and the first time I thought about suicide—with the world during my podcast interview on the Massachusetts General Hospital's Charged podcast. I knew if I shared my story, then maybe someone listening would get the courage to get help and no longer suffer in silence. I remember after recording that episode I was nervous for weeks that maybe I shared too much and maybe if a future employer heard the podcast, they would not hire me. All that anxiety was crushed when for months after the podcast episode was released, I received direct messages, emails, and texts from family, friends, bosses, colleagues, and complete strangers about how they connected with my message. Strangers were sharing stories of their struggles with depression and people I never would have guessed dealt with depression thanked me for my courage. I was and still am overwhelmed by the support, love, and thanks I received from so many people. This was my biggest lesson in using my platform: use it to touch lives.

We must use our privilege to advocate for the voiceless. To humanize our professions. To speak up on controversial topics that affect our families, friends, trainees, and patients. To speak up for marginalized individuals. To speak up for the neglected individuals in our communities and world. To speak up for those still building the courage to speak up for themselves. To speak about topics considered taboo—like mental health in academia. To speak up so that others feel brave enough to do so as well. Earlier I said that I love LeBron James. I admire him not only because he is the best basketball player of all time or because he built a school in Akron, Ohio, but because he uses his privilege and his platform to speak on social justice matters without fear of repercussion (like losing endorsements).

Work on your confidence by healing your mind, body, and soul first. Confident living means living life on your own terms, living authentically, and living a life of purpose. It means living fearlessly. With confidence comes courage. Regardless of the field you are in, when given a platform or blessed with privilege, use it for good. Your voice is needed.

1. Work on your confidence by healing your mind, body, and soul. Find the things that make you feel the least confident and work on them in manageable pieces. For example, if public speaking scares you, start with consistently speaking up at work meetings.

2. Build the courage to share your losses with the world too. It humanizes you and lets the world around you realize that success is not without failure. In sharing your losses, you will touch innumerable lives.

3. Use your platform and privilege to make the world a better place.

4. Love yourself deeply.

SPARK Notes

_____

_____

_____

_____

_____

_____

_____

_____

_____

_____

_____

_____

_____

_____

_____

_____

_____

_____

_____

_____

_____

_____

_____

_____

_____

_____

_____

_____

GRATITUDE

On the first day of my advanced heart failure and transplant cardiology fellowship my program director, Dr. Andreas Brieke, said that the year of training ahead of me would change me. I thought *yeah, okay, whatever.* Boy was I wrong. That year completely changed how I look at the world and how I live my life.

Heart transplant is truly a miracle, it is the circle of life— one soul is lost to allow another soul to live on. It was during this year of training that I was faced with the extremes of life and death. On the one hand I am hearing the story of the donor, someone who oftentimes was a young person who died unexpectedly. Whether it was an accident, an unintentional drug overdose, or suicide, it was heartbreaking. Death is always tragic, but when it is an unexpected or preventable death, it is even more tragic. I formed a picture in my mind of what the donor may have looked like, what they loved doing, what they struggled with, who they left behind, and how crushed their loved ones must be. And then after I have examined the heart and the rest of the medical data, I decide whether or not the donor heart is a suitable match for one of the patients on our list who has end-stage heart failure and has failed all medical and surgical options and is waiting for a second chance at life. If the heart is a good match, I get to call one of the patients waiting on the transplant list and tell them to grab their bags and head into the hospital, we "found" a heart for them. On the other end of that phone, almost always, I hear tears full of gratitude. The circle of life, right before my eyes.

How did that year change my life? Well, hearing the tragic stories of lives lost too early made me realize that the most important thing in this world is human connection. I stopped sweating the small stuff and stopped worrying about things I could not control. I started living life with intention. I started being more kind and forgiving. I realized that truly everyone is struggling in one way or another. I learned to love souls and not material things. Every time I get a call for a donor heart, I am reminded of how short life is and how important it is to live it authentically and to stay connected with the people I love. The donor stories reminded me to check in on friends and family I have lost touch with and to let go of old grudges. The deaths reminded me that experiences matter more than things. That the time I spend with my family or the girls' trip I decided to take to spend time with my best friends is more valuable than that Fendi bag or Louboutin pumps. The things that riled me up before no longer phased me. Now I live life fully, love deeply, and try my best to be kind and forgiving.

We have a great deal to be grateful for that we do not even realize the magnitude of our blessings until we stop to really think about them. I read a lot about the benefits of gratitude including improving mental well-being, happiness, and improving confidence—all the same things we talked about above. I have made a daily habit to write at least one thing I am grateful for every day, and I include it in my morning routine along with meditation, journaling, and exercising. The more specific you are about what you are grateful for, the better. So instead of saying, "I am grateful for my friends," write down the name of the friend you are grateful for and why you are grateful to have them in your life. We all have something to be grateful for each day. It could be as simple as waking up with a roof over our head and not worrying about where our next meal is coming from.

We have so much we ought to be grateful for, so take the time to be thankful for your blessings. I am beyond blessed, and every time I pick up the phone to hear about a donor heart and read about their life that was tragically lost, I remember to be grateful. A life that was so young, a life that had so much more to go, family and friends that were left behind. I am constantly reminded that I have a world of things to be grateful for and that everything can change at a moment's notice. Remember, struggle is relative, but many of the things that stress us out are truly not worth it.

What a blessing it is to be a small part of this circle of life. My program director was right: That year of training truly changed my life forever. Write down the things you are grateful for and put dates next to them. It is always fun to come back and look at the things you wrote down months, even years, later. And remember, gratitude increases your spiritual capital.

SPARK Suggestions

1. Make a habit of remembering everything you are blessed with during times when you feel like you do not have enough.

2. Remember that the connections and experiences are more meaningful than the things. Life is short, and it is certainly not guaranteed.

3. Write down at least one thing you are grateful for each day. Be specific.

4. Love yourself deeply.

SPARK Notes

_____

_____

_____

_____

_____

_____

_____

_____

_____

_____

_____

_____

_____

_____

_____

_____

_____

_____

_____

_____

_____

_____

CHAPTER 3

HUMAN SPARK

HUMAN CONNECTIONS

I previously mentioned human connections briefly, but I truly think they are the most valuable, precious, and important focus in our lives. In medicine, I have the opportunity to interact with many people—to create many connections. In turn, I see how patients rely on their human connections in their times of needs. One of the saddest moments to witness in medicine is a patient who is alone, with no family or friends to take care of them in their darkest time. These difficulties are compounded when we must turn down a patient for transplant because they have no one to support them through the post-transplant period.

While material things, including our most cherished accomplishments, are fleeting, the connections we build with people are not. I know that not everyone we meet is meant to be in our lives forever, but everyone we meet has something they can teach us. No two people are the same—we all have different life journeys and different perspectives. Learn something from everyone you cross paths with. Everyone has something to teach the world, we just have to take a moment to listen and appreciate it, and we do not always do that.

Because of my career, I face the extremes of life and death regularly. That experience is what has taught me to cherish human connections. Sometimes we get so wrapped up in our careers that we lose sight of this super important thing. We get super busy building our empires that we forget to connect with our families and friends. We forget to connect with our spouses and partners on a level other than the usual taking care of the house and family way. I keep saying it, but I mean it, what makes life special are the connections and the experiences, not the things. We all have dreams and goals we are working to crush, myself included, and that is spectacular, but we cannot forget the human connections along the way.

I find the best interactions I have with patients are the ones where I connect with them on a human level and not a disease level. Of course, we must discuss heart disease for that is why they are seeing me in clinic, but tell me what ignites that fire inside you? Who are you? What matters to you? What do you love to do? Who are the important people in your life? What are you worried about? What are you scared of? When are you the happiest? What is your favorite thing in the whole wide world? And the way patients light up when we talk about the things most important to them lets me know I connected with them on a human level and I made it known to them that I care about them outside of their disease as well.

The beauty of the world lies in the connections we make with others. My advice to you is to not lose yourself in your career so much that you forget about the world and people outside of it. Remember that hobby you loved before you got incredibly busy? Find a club that you can join to connect with others who love that hobby just as much as you do and make time for it. Those friends you keep canceling on because you are writing a paper or grading exams? Make time for brunch, dinner, or drinks with them at least once a month. The family member we sometimes take for granted? Pick up the phone and call or invite them over for dinner or a holiday celebration—or just say hello. And for your own family, make sure you are present in your children and partner's life, if you have either. Be present in every activity or event you are invited to attend—and stop turning down invitations. The work will always be there, but these connections, experiences, and people will not. And importantly, if you are in a relationship, start dating again. Make time once a week to go on a date, ignite that love and excitement again.

Oprah Winfrey says, "Be interested, not interesting." Try to really understand people, ask them questions rather than talking only about yourself. When your mental, physical, and spiritual health is aligned, you have more self-confidence and self-love that you do not always have to talk about yourself and can devote your energy to others. But you also gain that health, love, and confidence by devoting your energy to others—it goes both ways.

Remember, the material things—the awards, the promotions, the corner office—are all great things, but the most beautiful things about this crazy life are the human connections we make. Cherish them. Make time for them. Nurture them.

1. Connect with a friend you have been thinking about but because it has been so long you have been embarrassed to reach out. Send a text, an email, or make a call. It will be so worth it.

2. Add "dates" with friends, family, your significant other, and your children (as applicable) to your calendar. Schedule these on a weekly or monthly basis, just like you schedule things for school or work.

3. Remember that most material things are fleeting. Cherish the experiences and the human connections.

4. Love yourself deeply.

SPARK Notes

NETWORKING

Networking can be hard, especially when you are early in your career and may not feel confident, but once you start doing it, it becomes much easier. Early in your career—or after experiencing a change in careers—you may feel like you have nothing to offer people because you are inexperienced in the field, so why would anyone want to speak with you? Networking is not about connecting with job titles. It is about connecting with people. You may not have the most experience, the fanciest title, or the highest degree, but you are a human with much to offer, just like anyone else in that room.

For those in careers with professional organizations that hold regular conferences, make sure to attend as many as you can. I personally go to conferences for the networking and socializing more than the learning. I can learn any time, but conferences are the ideal place to connect with people with similar career and social interests. I make a point to attend the social events or sessions where you can walk around and talk to people with interests like yours. These allow you to create deeper, more meaningful connections than events like speed mentoring, where there are time limits on your interaction with each person.

It is not only important to connect with people at the event but also to follow up with them after the event. Always send an email re-introducing yourself, thanking them for a great conversation, and offering to be of service if they need you in the future. However, do not be suffocating. Reach out once or twice, but if you do not hear back, simply move on. Even more important is the understanding that networking is a two-way street, both parties should benefit from the relationship. While walking up to people and chatting them up can seem daunting, most people are flattered that you find their work interesting and want to speak to them more about it. Make sure when you connect with people that it is not just a selfish thing on your part, but that you have something to offer the person you connected with as well, even if it is small. Be genuine, and you should not have any problems.

We are discussing networking after mind, body, and soul health and confidence and courage for a reason. You need all of those to effectively network. The task will not seem so daunting if you are feeling great about yourself. Networking will become fun when you change your mindset from it being something work-related to an opportunity to meet new people, hear new perspectives, and learn new information. It really is fun to meet people doing things you have an interest in and even more fun when your personalities jive.

Why is networking critically important—so important that it is mentioned along with your mind, body, and soul health? Because it is necessary for growth and elevation. Networking opens a whole different world to you where people may do things differently than you are used to—whether that is at your workplace or in your personal life. Networking may lead to new career opportunities, open doors to new research or social justice initiatives, or be the reason you are invited to chair a committee, sit on a board, get promoted, or become a member of a prestigious organization. Effective networking can change the trajectory of your career and your life. Networking can also lead to long-term relationships and result in a mentoring or sponsoring type of relationship (or a friendship!). Both are equally important for personal and career development.

Other than networking in-person at meetings, social media is an effective tool to grow your connection pool. I have met colleagues, some of who became friends, on Twitter because we share career and social interests. They have invited me to co-author papers and to speak at their institutions and, in turn, I have invited them to do the same. Again, networking is a relationship where both parties benefit. It is always awesome when I get to see the colleagues and friends in my field in real life at conferences after we have met on social media. My ability to network has opened doors for me that have directly contributed to my career and personal growth. And while Twitter is the preferred social media platform for many academic cardiologists, you can find out where peers in your field are active and go connect with them there!

And when I say connect, I mean actively participate. Do not get on social media and just lurk. You will never meet anyone that way. Share the work you are proud of, promote your mentees and trainees, connect with like-minded colleagues, post, advocate, and engage. The world will never know how great you are until you share your gifts and passions with it. And you should not be arrogant or humble brag, but if you are sharing your accomplishments because you are genuinely proud of them, the intention will be clear.

Do not be shy. Get out there and network. Register for your major conferences and network in real life. Find the social media platform popular in your field and get on there and network virtually. Most importantly, nurture those relationships, remember that for effective networking both parties should benefit, and finally, be genuine, authentic, and humble in all you do.

SPARK Suggestions

1. Register for the next major conference in your field and go there with the mindset of networking and building connections. Once you are there, attend all the networking and social events scheduled and walk around in poster areas or lounges where you can walk up and introduce yourself to someone you admire in your field. You got this!

2. Find out which social media is most popular in your field and create an account. Make sure you have an updated headshot and a clear (and fun) bio. Connect with others in your field or outside of it that you respect and admire. Post, engage, and check back regularly.

3. Always, always, always be genuine, be authentic, and be humble in all your networking adventures.

4. Love yourself deeply.

SPARK Notes

MENTORS, SPONSORS, AND COACHES

If you are reading this book, you probably know the difference between a mentor, sponsor, and coach. But just in case: A mentor is someone who tells you what you need to do to succeed or attain a specific goal. A sponsor puts you in the position to succeed. And a coach is someone who brings out the very best talent inside of you and with that, helps you achieve your goals. All are different and all three are critical to success. I have benefited tremendously from my mentors, sponsors, and coaches. My personal and career development would not be where it is without them. A person can be both a mentor and sponsor depending on the situation and they can also be a coach to others. I play all three roles for different people in my life. One thing I will stress is that we all reached a certain level of success because someone saw something in us that we had not yet seen in ourselves, so we have to pay it forward to the generations coming after us. Especially to marginalized students and trainees who often do not have access to the same opportunities others do.

It is extremely important to not only have more than one mentor, sponsor, and coach but to also have different guides for different areas of your life. I have career mentors and sponsors and life mentors; both serve different roles. It is also important that you have career mentors and sponsors who have no vested interest in you. Of course, everyone should have your best interest at heart, but we are all only human and this world can be cruel as you are aware. So sometimes you might need career advice from someone whose promotion or publication track record, for example, is not connected to you in anyway. Nurture those relationships as well. Some mentors and sponsors will want to meet with you regularly, whereas others may only want to meet on an as-needed basis.

These relationships work best when not only career interests are similar, but when life and social interests are similar too. Then, there is a human connection other than the work at hand. There must be a professional and personal spark. When research or work interests are similar but there is no human connection, I find that it is hard to develop a successful mentor-mentee relationship. Set boundaries and know your own boundaries. Remember that mentors, sponsors, and coaches care about you very much, but they are not your friends (although some may become your friends later)! Respect their time. Come prepared. Send succinct emails. Do not expect responses in evenings or weekends if matters are not urgent. Show up to every opportunity afforded you and trust me, more will keep coming.

Never burn bridges and never ghost your mentor, sponsor, or coach. If the relationship is not working because you have very different working styles or there is no human connection, then let them know. Most are incredibly busy and understand if you need to find someone you connect with better. Always respect the relationship. The world is small, and the more specialized your field is, the smaller the world is. Your reputation is the key to a fruitful and satisfying career. Which is why you must show up in everything you do every single time. The better job you do with an opportunity, the more your mentor or sponsor will send your way.

Finally, make a conscious effort to pay it forward. Just like your mentors, sponsors, and coaches saw something in you that you had not seen in yourself, you can do the same for someone else. Everyone needs support to reach the highest echelons of their career. You should reach out and support the quiet ones, the shy ones, the underrepresented minorities, and the women in your field among many others who are often voiceless in the boardrooms. We owe it to the generations behind us. Importantly, you have to devote enough time to your mentees and to ensure you are not overloading yourself with mentees because the relationship is only impactful when you can dedicate time to nurturing it.

Make time to mentor the next generation of scientists, clinicians, artists, lawyers, teachers, electricians, and chefs. We owe it to future generations who will hopefully continue to make this world a better place and in return, mentor the generation following them. And lastly, I did not think I needed to say it, but I do, based on what I have seen on Twitter. Mentoring is for free! Do not pay anyone to mentor you, for every person charging fees for mentoring, there are 100 people who do it because they were mentored for free and just love doing it. Do not get roped into that scam.

SPARK Suggestions

1. Identify mentors and sponsors at your company or institution and others in other companies. Make sure you connect on a professional and human level. Nurture the relationship.

2. Think about getting a coach—a career coach, a life coach, a business coach, etc. Their role is different than the role of a mentor or sponsor. Coaches bring out the best in you. I have a leadership coach, Mr. Jim McKenna, who has been instrumental in my career and personal growth.

3. Pay it forward! Mentor and sponsor more junior people in or interested in your field and make sure you devote time to their development. Do not agree to mentor or sponsor more people than your schedule allows.

4. Love yourself deeply.

SPARK Notes

SOCIAL JUSTICE

The last and most important part of the Human Spark is social justice. Each one of us must play a role in ensuring the communities around us have equitable access to the resources in our field. For what are we if we do not fight for the communities around us. For me, this is healthcare. While healthcare should be a basic human right, in the United States it is a privilege because of the way our healthcare system is set up. In turn, every healthcare worker has the duty to fight the systems and politics in place that have made healthcare inaccessible to disadvantaged communities. How will we ever explain to our children, grandchildren, and the generation after them that we allow some people to die because they cannot afford medications? From insulin to heart transplant, people die in the United States simply because they cannot afford to pay for medications; even with insurance coverage, co-payments are often unaffordable. That $60 co-payment may not mean much to an executive of a Fortune 500 company, but it may mean a decision between groceries for the week or a necessary medication for someone less privileged. The absolute worst part of being a transplant physician—and this is true of transplant in the United States, not just any particular institution—is turning down a patient for transplant simply because they cannot afford to pay for the post-transplant care and medications. It is gut-wrenching and inhumane. It is traumatizing. What about the health of undocumented immigrants? Refugees? Prisoners? They are human beings too, right? And they deserve the world class healthcare offered to billionaires, but in our current healthcare system that just does not happen.

I am not a health policy expert and I do not pretend to be one, but I am obligated to do what I can to raise awareness and disrupt racist systems in place that contribute to these horrible inequities. The kind of "good trouble" the late, great Congressman John Lewis spoke of often. There are inequities in every specialty in medicine and the one that is closest to my heart is the inequity in organ allocation in heart transplant. So, what am I going to do about it? Well, I and many others are tired of reading research papers about the inequities. It is now the time—and has been for over 400 years—to disrupt the racist systems contributing to those inequities. We must go into Black and brown communities and earn trust, form relationships, and establish clinics to evaluate patients with end-stage heart disease who need heart transplant. Most importantly, we need to involve the communities we want to reach in these efforts to meet their needs. The earning of trust and relationships will take time, but it is the most crucial step to ensure efforts to dismantle systemic racism contributing to grave inequities in heart transplant are successful.

Inequities exist in every field, from law to education, and it is critical for those who have achieved success to look around them and identify the inequities and ways to dismantle systems contributing to them. Every one of us has the duty to dismantle systemic inequity in every field we are in. Look around the room and see what you can do to change things. Small steps lead to bigger wins in the future. We must use our voices and privilege to make room for the poor, disadvantaged, neglected, and forgotten souls among us. Use your power to ignite change. I mentioned before how much I admire LeBron James for using his platform to financially support and speak out against systemic racism from police brutality to voter suppression. Get involved.

You really can change the world by changing just one life. Imagine meeting a young Black high school student at a career fair who tells you he is interested in becoming a cardiac surgeon? What if you mentor, sponsor, and coach him through college, medical school, residency, and fellowship and then one day he becomes a heart transplant surgeon who saves countless lives? That is how you change the world. One person at a time.

Do not take it from me, take it from a legend we lost and who the world barely deserved, one of my heroes Congressman John Lewis. As he would say, go on out and stir up some "good trouble." The world desperately needs your courage.

SPARK Suggestions

1. Use your privilege and your platform to speak out against social injustice.

2. Stir up "good trouble" that dismantles systems of oppression.

3. Remember, when you are doing what it is best for humanity, you are never wrong. Think outside of your bubble, think of the poorest, sickest, and most neglected among us.

4. Love yourself deeply.

SPARK Notes

CHAPTER 4

CAREER SPARK

IMPOSTER SYNDROME

My first experience with imposter syndrome happened when I moved to Boston. I felt like a fraud. I felt like I was not good enough, that I was not smart enough, that I did not belong. I was so afraid someone would one day realize they made a mistake in hiring me. It was in the beginning of my third fellowship in clinical cardiology research at an Ivy League institution surrounded by some of the most brilliant minds in my field. It seemed that everyone had either attended an Ivy League medical school or trained at an Ivy League residency or fellowship program, and here I was, a girl from Ohio, who went to a state college and medical school and did not train at a fancy residency or program. I did not think I was good enough to be there despite knowing I was extremely well trained. My imposter syndrome was awful, it contributed to my deep depression. I remember an older male colleague asking me a medical question sarcastically once saying "Is that how they taught you to do it in Cincinnati?" and ooh wee, how that got to me. It was a way to further make me feel a lack of belonging. But now understand that a comment like that is a projection of that person's insecurity. It was rare for others to make me feel like I did not deserve to be there, but the insecurity stemmed from me. I had to dig deep inside and find my confidence again, and I had to remember that I was there for a reason. One of my attendings in Denver, Dr. JoAnn Lindenfeld, saw something in me that I had yet to see in myself and sent me to Boston where my fellowship program director/mentor/sponsor Dr. Jim Januzzi nurtured that confidence and was instrumental in launching my career.

I picked up a book called *The Confidence Code* by Katty Kay and Claire Shipman and was floored to find out that many highly successful women and men dealt with imposter syndrome. I even read somewhere that the late great Dr. Maya Angelou dealt with imposter syndrome too and spoke about how one day people would discover she was a fraud. Senators, chief executives, and lawyers alike, all speak of their experiences with imposter syndrome. I think woman, especially Black and brown women (and men), experience imposter syndrome the higher they get on the career ladder. Why? Because the boardroom and C-suites lack people who look like them. Because sometimes those very people make us feel like we do not belong. The feeling of not belonging is one of the most destructive feelings to experience.

I heard the co-founder of Black Lives Matter, Ms. Alicia Garza, say she is a survivor of imposter syndrome. A powerful woman who ignited a world-changing movement also suffered imposter syndrome, and now she considers herself a survivor. Not many people talk about the bumps along their journey to success, but when they do, it undoubtedly helps so many that listen to their story. I would not say I am an imposter syndrome survivor yet, because it still creeps in from time to time, but I am able to crush it and take the opportunity I am given and perform at my highest level.

Though my first and worst experience with imposter syndrome was when I moved to Boston, there have been times when I have been invited to give a talk or sit on a committee that I never dreamed of and I immediately wonder if I am established in my career enough, good enough, or smart enough to be there. Well, someone saw something in me and believed I deserved this opportunity, so you know what? I damn sure deserve to be in those rooms, at those tables, and in those seats. I must believe in myself more than anyone else believes in me to reach my highest level of success.

When you have your Health Spark, your Life Spark, and your Human Spark in order, it becomes harder for imposter syndrome to overwhelm you. I have found that it sneaks in less and less and when I do feel surprised about an opportunity that comes my way because it is something that excites me, or that I have wanted for so long, or something that I am passionate about, I stop and thank God for the good and blessings in disguise that brought me to this point. Regardless of whether I feel like I deserve something, or if an opportunity freaks me out because it seems so huge, I prepare and I show up like it was made for me. Be confident yet remain humble and opportunities will continue to present themselves to you.

My first experience with imposter syndrome contributed to my depression and anxiety. And sometimes imposter syndrome can be bad enough that you may need a licensed therapist to help you deal with it. If that is the case, take action because it can be an impediment to your continued career and personal development. I have found looking at the facts helps me crush my imposter syndrome when it creeps in. I remind myself that the things I have accomplished are the reason I am met with these incredible opportunities. One of my funniest experiences with imposter syndrome was when several people called or email to ensure I was going to attend the cardiology fellows' graduation and I thought about not going because I thought I was going to get pranked. Little did I know, they gave me a teaching award! I could not believe it and did not believe I deserved the award. I kept asking the fellows, why did you give me this? I do not teach in a classroom. They said, teaching is not just teaching in a classroom, it is your mentoring, your sponsoring, and how you are a role model to us. To this day, it is the only "medical" thing I have hanging up in my office, the rest is artwork.

So, remember that some of the most successful people have dealt with imposter syndrome. The more successful you become, the more likely you will have to deal with it. Do not let it stop you. Learn ways to crush it by working on your Health, Life, and Human Spark or get professional help if you need to. And be encouraged: Ms. Alicia Garza said she is an imposter syndrome survivor! You deserve to occupy the spaces you are invited to be in.

SPARK Suggestions

1. Read the book *The Confidence Code* by Katty Kay and Claire Shipman to learn more about imposter syndrome and the super successful people who have dealt with it.

2. Identify the times in your life and/or career where you have dealt with imposter syndrome and think about why it happened, what the internal contributors were, and what the external forces were.

3. Focus on the facts. Your concrete past successes are the reason you are continuing to soar. If you need help crushing imposter syndrome, seek professional help from a licensed therapist.

4. Love yourself deeply.

SPARK Notes

SETTING BOUNDARIES AND IDENTIFYING PRIORITIES

Boundaries are critically important to personal and career development. Why? Because no one can do everything. You must prioritize things in your life and career. When someone is successful and multi-talented, they frequently become the go-to person for everyone in their family, their circle of friends, and at work. You know what trying to do everything for everyone results in? Burnout. When your family calls you for medical advice, career advice, or to solve every family argument, it can get exhausting. When your friends know you are good at something and call you to help them make a website, call you to ask you to opine on the health of their sick aunt, or ask you to volunteer your time for their non-profits, that can get exhausting too. And when everyone at works realizes you are efficient and work hard, they ask you to do everything, sit on every committee, and represent your division or team at every meeting. Also, incredibly exhausting. Having no boundaries is also a result of low self-confidence, wanting to people-please, and being worried about what happens when you say no.

You cannot do it all. And you should not. It is important to show up and show out in everything you do. Whether it is to co-author a paper, coach a team, or sit on a committee because your reputation is at stake. You should only agree to get involved with things that you have the time for and know you will do well, otherwise you will not be able to truly show up and do your best. I really dislike sitting on committees or being given titles where I am not contributing anything. I prefer not to occupy my time with anything for the sake of putting it on my resume. As we know, time is valuable and life is short. Transplant patients remind me of this on an almost daily basis. Anything you do, strive to do well. Your work represents you. It represents your personal brand, and you do not want an opportunity that does not align with your purpose. It would waste your time where you can spend it doing something meaningful and, if you do not do it well because you do not want to put forth the effort, it could tarnish your reputation. A strong personal brand is the key to a successful and happy career. It is priceless.

Early in my career it was hard to say no to anything. I was a brand-new attending and I wanted to impress everyone—to prove to them I deserved to be there. In hindsight, I do think it was important to say yes to every opportunity in the beginning because I had not yet figured out exactly what I wanted to do with my life despite many years of school and training. Doing everything allowed me to realize what I loved, liked, and barely tolerated. Doing everything also connected me with many people from so many different specialties. But it became exhausting. Because I wanted to do everything I picked up to the best of my ability, and I find you have to put even more energy into doing things you do not actually like. So, the networking and building human connections piece was incredible, but I could not go on doing work I had no interest in.

Now, when presented with an opportunity, I ask for time to think about it before eagerly jumping in and saying yes. And then I consider if the opportunity falls into one of my five P's: pay, promote, push, passion, and purpose. I ask myself will this opportunity **Pay** me. I make sure to ask if there is a budget for the opportunity and find out what my white male colleagues are getting paid. If you do not ask, you will never get it. I also ask myself will this opportunity **Promote** me. For those of us in academia, we know there are certain requirements necessary to advance from assistant to associate to full professor and similar milestones exist for other fields. I also ask myself will this opportunity **Push** me. Meaning, will this opportunity push me to learn something new that I have been afraid to learn, will it push me out of my comfort zone and help me grow. I ask myself am I **Passionate** about this opportunity. Is it something I love doing, and would I do it for free because it enriches my life, like mentoring or health advocacy? I also ask myself does this opportunity align with my **Purpose.** That speaks for itself. We all have a purpose on this earth and opportunities that present themselves to us are the best when they align with our purpose.

Once you learn to discern your priorities, learn how to manage your time and stay organized. I took a class senior year of college—after I was already accepted into medical school and was partying for a year straight. It was called "Time Management," and I ended up finding it useful, even though I signed up for the class as a joke. My entire life is on my Google calendar, everything from work meetings, patients I am seeing in clinic to dates with friends, eyebrow-threading appointments, manicures, and galas. I do not show up to anything unless it is on my calendar. I have a notepad with the heading "Shit to Do" on each page that has all the tasks I want to complete in a particular month. I am old school in that regard. I love the feeling of crossing things off on my notepad. And finally, I have Post-Its that I place on my desk or laptop for the tasks that need to be completed that day. I love the gratification of pulling a Post-It off my desk and throwing it in the recycling bin. This is how I stay organized. Find a system that works for you.

I recommend saying yes to everything in the beginning of your career when you are still figuring out what you want to do. But when you do figure that out, create a system which helps you decide which opportunities you are going to say yes to. Find a way to get and stay organized. And remember to set boundaries with family, friends, and colleagues. Your time is precious, and you want to put energy into the things that are truly meaningful to your life.

SPARK Suggestions

1. Create and communicate boundaries with family, friends, and colleagues. Your time is precious.

2. Create a system that helps you decide which opportunities you are going to say yes to. My 5 Ps are: Pay me? Promote me? Push me? Passionate about it? Align with my Purpose?

3. Bring your best self to every opportunity afforded you. A great reputation is the key to a fulfilling career.

4. Love yourself deeply.

SPARK Notes

LEADING WITH GRACE AND AUTHENTICITY

Bosses. We have all had them. Good ones, great ones, and some terrible ones. I always thought I learned the most from the great bosses I have had, but I realize I learn even more from the not-so-hot ones. I learn exactly what not to do when I lead a division, department, and hospital one day. I have read so many books on leadership and listened to so many podcasts. I have also watched YouTube videos, listened to TED Talks, and attended leadership courses. My most valuable leadership training experience has been my one-on-one leadership coaching. I remember meeting with the chair of my department, Dr. Katrina Armstrong. She told me I needed to make sure I was not being overcoached, a concept she said was more common in women. I make it clear to my leadership coach that, throughout this process, I never want to lose the essence of me; I just want to be the best version of myself. I also never want to sound rehearsed, like some bosses do.

A valuable exercise was taking a personality test to better understand my leadership style. I have taken so many of those tests and they all tell me about myself—that I am driven, stubborn, lack patience, and persuasive, among other characteristics. Some I am extremely proud of, others not so much. I find that the leadership moments I am least proud of are the ones where I have said something in the heat of the moment that may have really hurt someone. Those instances helped me realize that my words are powerful and that I never want to use my words to break anyone down. Even more valuable has been learning how to interact with people who fall in completely opposite parts of the pie. By sharing stories of leadership situations, I am proud of and others that mortify me, my coach helps me understand how others function and how I can be the best leader I can be. For example, while I and others may feel comfortable blurting out suggestions or answers in the middle of a work meeting with no heads up, others may need notice regarding the agenda of the meeting and that their opinion may be solicited.

The leadership coaching I have received has been invaluable to my growth and has opened my eyes to the sometimes horrific leadership present in academia. I think everyone who wants to run a division, department, or company needs a leadership coach. There are many personalities to manage that I cannot imagine doing so without formal training. I do believe some people are born leaders, and some people have no interest at all in leadership positions; either way, a formal leadership position should require leadership coaching. We must demand better leaders.

Throughout my leadership coaching, my idea of what makes a great leader has evolved. At first, I said I want to be the leader everyone aspires to be but now I believe the greatest leaders are the ones who make everyone around them the best version of themselves. And that is the leader I will work to become. An authentic and transformational leader, with the ability to change people's lives by bringing out the best in them is the leader I aspire to be. I plan to continue my leadership coaching because it has been an integral part of my career and personal development. Leadership coaching is expensive, but there are great books you can read and courses you can attend about leadership. My recommendation for the next time you re-negotiate your contract, start a new position, or are given a leadership position is to request a budget for leadership coaching. Your division, department, or company will be more successful as a whole because of it and the people working with you will be much happier.

Company culture starts at the top, so taking the time to coach leaders makes for a better environment for all. Happier employees produce more which in turn benefits the institution or company's bottom line. We all know the bosses we do not want to be like, so let us work on being the bosses who change the culture of our institutions and organizations. When I picture myself in a leadership position, I have the following vision: My team will be happy; my team will feel appreciated; my team will feel like they are contributing to the greater good; my team will respect each other even if they do not like each other; my team will be the best version of themselves; my team will feel supported; my team will feel like they are one big work family, even if it is a dysfunctional one; and my team will enjoy working in whatever organization I direct. I have read that even one bad apple can destroy the culture of an entire team so I would make sure that such toxic personalities, if not remedial, are gone. At least that is how I picture it.

Great leaders change lives. Be the leader who changes lives.

SPARK Suggestions

1. If you are considering a leadership position, request formal leadership coaching. My leadership coach is Mr. Jim McKenna, and he is fantastic.

2. Read books and articles on leadership or attend a course. Find out if your institution has formal leadership training and request to be trained. You can also pick up the biography of a leader you aspire to be and learn about their leadership style. Coach K (Mike Krzyzewski) is an extraordinary leader which you can read about or watch his interviews. I have learned so much by reading about his leadership style.

3. Take a test to determine your leadership style and read tips on how you can best manage those with leadership styles different than yours. It will be an incredibly eye-opening experience.

4. Love yourself deeply.

SPARK Notes

BUILDING A BADASS LEGACY

We all want to leave the world a better place long after we are gone. What kind of legacy do you want to build? Do you want to leave a legacy that leaves the world of science and medicine a better place? Do you want to leave a legacy that has touched the lives of numerous people? Or have you not thought about it? What I want people to say long after my death is that I made their lives better, that I empowered them to be the best version of themselves, and that I changed some people's lives. The published papers, professorships, books, and international talks are all great accolades, but the mark I want to leave on this earth has to do with human connections.

Take some time to think about what it is you want to leave behind and if the career or position you are in right now is truly where you want to be. Ponder what you would be doing if money were not a concern and figure out how you can do exactly that and get paid for it so you can pay your bills. Successful people are often already looking ahead at the next goal they want to tackle before pausing and relishing in the goals they have already crushed. I know I am guilty of that. Something seems so out of reach and is extremely exciting, but once I get it, I say oh, okay, no big deal, what's next? I have had to teach myself to cherish and celebrate every win. I must congratulate myself and acknowledge the hard work it took for me to get that win. It is the reason I throw an outrageous birthday party for myself every year.

Every year since I became an attending physician (and was no longer a broke trainee!) I throw a huge birthday party for myself. I invite my closest friends and family who come from all over the country. It is always incredibly amazing to see people from different parts of my life come together and enjoy life for that moment. I look at these parties like a huge family reunion with dinner, drinks, and dancing,—a time to celebrate everything I accomplished that year. I rarely take the time to celebrate my wins and tend to dwell on my losses, though I have gotten much better at reversing this, it is still something I need to remind myself of. The losses are lessons. The losses are blessings in disguise. A door that did not open or an opportunity that did not become mine was just not meant to be. Not part of my incredible journey. I say this to say: Find a way to celebrate your wins before marking that checkbox and moving on to the next goal.

Sit down in a quiet place now and re-write another letter to yourself. But this time write it as though you were writing it to your best friend in the whole world. That way you will gas yourself up, be kind and forgiving to yourself, and show yourself love from the depths of your soul. Write a letter to yourself about how you will never let the dreams of the child inside of you die. Write about everything you have accomplished at school, in life, and in your career. Write about the people whose lives you impacted. Write about the people who have thanked you and you shrugged it off like it was nothing. Write about all the times you put yourself before others. Write about the time you were crazy enough to think you can change the world but how you truly did. Write about how your mentees and the people you sponsored have succeeded underneath your leadership. Write about how you poured love into the universe. Write about how you made the world a better place by simply existing. I want you to write this letter to remind yourself of how much you have done and how much your presence here on earth is cherished because of the countless ways you have made the world better. Keep this letter next to your nightstand.

This is how you decide how it is you want to be remembered. This is how you decide how it is you want to leave your mark on this world. Remember, the impact you have on people will live on long after you are gone. By living your best life, living life on your own terms, defining success how you see it, and not taking any moment for granted, you empower everyone around you to do the same. And how amazing would it be to have left the world a happier, healthier, and more content place?

SPARK Suggestions

1. Celebrate your wins before moving onto your next goal. Relish the moments. You worked hard for them.

2. Decide what legacy you want to leave behind and be intentional about incorporating that into your life and career.

3. The impact you have had on people will last long after you are gone. Be kind, be forgiving, be inspirational, and be transformational.

4. Love yourself deeply.

SPARK Notes

CHAPTER 5

MONEY SPARK

FINANCIAL GOALS

Money can be a taboo topic. I know I do not feel comfortable talking about it. It seems like such a tacky thing to do. Let me digress for a second here and tell you how money has been the reason I have dumped some men. Either they were too cheap and expected me to pay for everything or they were so insecure, all they talked about was how much money they made or the money-making potential they had. Ooh wee, next! I always joke with my best friend that if I ever run into those men again, I will ask for my money back. Okay, back to money. It may be uncomfortable, but we must talk about it here! I saved it for the end where it belongs. Like my brother Mostafa and I discussed: After the Health Spark, the Life Spark, and the Human Spark are in order then comes the Career Spark and then the Money Spark. You cannot have the career and money, without having those first three in order, he said. He is wise beyond his years. I should call him Money Moose (Moose is his nickname). But, I digress.

Money is power, and it makes the world go round. Women are paid less than men, and Black and Latinx women make even less than white women. It is tragic. Even when adjusted for everything, women still make less than men, by several fold! And it is not because we do not ask—it is true we need to work on asking for what we want and negotiating for ourselves more, but even when we do ask, we still get paid less than men. Additionally, Black and Latinx men get paid less than white men. So, the only ones winning in this money situation here are white men. And therefore, we must talk about money.

I remember a woman physician telling me she got a leadership position for an obstetrics and gynecology department, a field that is predominantly women, and when she reviewed the salaries of the staff in the department, she was shocked. Even in a field that is predominantly women, men in the department were getting paid more than the women. And the most shocking thing was, even men who worked fewer clinical hours than some of the women were getting paid more than them! We have to make salaries transparent and it cannot be on employees to ask for more; the people paying those employees need to be held accountable to ensure equitable payment between women and men—and between underrepresented professionals and those who dominate the field.

In the meantime, get comfortable with negotiating everything! Start with your compensation. Always ask for more—and more does not necessarily have to mean more money. It can mean more benefits (and those largely depend on the field you are in) or paid time off. Ask your white male colleagues to give you a range for what you should expect for a certain position. Ask for transparency from the people deciding your salary. When negotiating the salary for a job I thought I was going to take, I straight up asked the finance person discussing the proposed salary with me, "Is this what you would pay me if I were a white man?" He was shook. Practice negotiating in other aspects of your life and practice before you begin contract negotiations with a potential future employer. As with networking, both sides must benefit. Make a case, filled with fool-proof facts of why you deserve a raise, and even more importantly, how a raise or more support will help you help your institution or organization reap even more wins. Get comfortable asking for what you deserve.

Like we discussed in the previous section, stop saying yes to doing everything—and stop saying yes to doing everything for free. When invited to speak or sit on the board of an organization, ask them what the budget they put towards such opportunities is. If you do not ask the first time, people will assume you are always willing to do things for free, and they will keep coming back. Your time is valuable. Set a price for how much you charge per hour, and then estimate how much time you think you will spend on said opportunity, then ask for your money. I also started asking my male colleagues how much they charge per hour or per speaking event to make sure I am not low-balling myself. I am no financial expert, but I spend a lot of time reading about personal finance, because when I understand the basics of money—saving, investing, interest, budgeting, planning, and negotiating—I feel more confident.

Financial literacy is empowering. They do not teach us about finances in medical school, but I wish they did. Everything I learned, I learned from my dad and from the books I read. My favorite book on personal finance is *The Automatic Millionaire* by David Bach. This book may not be for everyone, but I love Bach's books because they are simple and clear, and they teach the basics, which is exactly what I wanted to know. Even knowing the basics has made a huge difference in my confidence and ability to talk about money, manage my money, and to ask for more money!

Set your financial goals. Take out a pen and piece of paper and write down where you want to see yourself financially in the next one, five, and ten years and beyond. Next, write down exactly how you plan on getting there. Goals without a plan are just dreams, as they say. Learn how to plan and budget. A clear plan, with actionable items, will get you where you need to be. Goals are crystallized when they are written down, so write down your financial goals, and be specific. Do not just write down you want to buy a house, write down when and where, write down how big it is, and visualize what that house will look like and how it will feel to live in it.

Learn about money. Take control of your money. Always ask for more. And certainly, write down your financial goals and how you plan on achieving them. Encourage your family members to learn about money management as well. Teach the youth in your communities how to manage money. Financial literacy can change the course of people's lives, and that is why we must talk about money.

 **SPARK Suggestions**

1. Take a class on the art of negotiation. It will help you feel more confident negotiating your salary and benefits and other money matters.

2. Never accept the first offer. Always ask for more. Ask your white male colleagues for a range of what you should expect to get paid.

3. Write down your financial goals and create a plan to achieve them. Goals without plans are just dreams.

4. Love yourself deeply.

SPARK Notes

_____

_____

_____

_____

_____

_____

_____

_____

_____

_____

_____

_____

_____

_____

_____

_____

_____

_____

_____

_____

_____

_____

_____

_____

_____

_____

PLANNING AND BUDGETING

I had a blessed upbringing and was privileged to always be supported by my parents until I started getting my own paycheck as a resident physician. Even now, whenever I need anything, they do not hesitate to help me. I can—and must—acknowledge my privilege. While residents get paid peanuts, those peanuts were enough for me to live comfortably…in Cincinnati! Fast forward to my move to Boston with those same peanuts, and I was broke out of my mind. This sounds bougie, but it was the first time I had to figure out how to budget and plan. I remember being shocked at how much more expensive deodorant and yogurt were and that I was paying what could be the mortgage of a nice house to live in a one-bedroom, ground-floor apartment, with a window air-conditioning unit. It was time for me to learn how to manage my money.

I sat down and looked at my bank statements and noted where I was spending most of my money—on Uber and on eating out. I then created a monthly budget. I wrote down my fixed costs—things like rent, electric, gym memberships, medical school loan payments, etc. Then I looked at what was left as "money to blow." It was not as much as I thought I had to spend indiscreetly, so I looked at where I could cut down spending. I knew it was not going to be my manicures and pedicures because those were how I treated myself, but I knew I could cut down on my eating out habits. I did not really start saving until I got my first "real" job.

Now when got my first "real" job as an attending physician, I decided I was going to enjoy not being broke for no more than a year then start budgeting again. I made sure I was making maximum contributions to my retirement plan and that money was coming directly out of my paycheck without me seeing it, so it did not exist to me. This is the whole "pay yourself first" concept in action. I had my same fixed costs column and "money to blow" column but now I had additional buckets. I had short-term savings bucket for international trips or big expenses and an investment bucket. I have a rainy-day fund if, God forbid, I were to lose my job. That fund would last me a year. I know that sounds paranoid, but most sources say to have enough to support you for three to six months. I also have a fund for future child-bearing costs I may incur such as in vitro fertilization or adoption. Knowing where my money came from and what I was doing with it each month made me feel confident. Financial literacy is empowering, and women should be part of the financial game as much as men are.

I believe everyone should learn the basics of money management, even if you have a partner that manages the money for your household. What if something happens to them? You should know where the money is and where it is invested. And my opinion on sharing everything is simple: Do not do it. People always say, what if your future husband gets sick of you? I say, what if I get sick of him first? I am keeping my finances separate. I think money causes a lot of stress in relationships, so talk about it openly and talk about it early.

Financial security is also important for confidence. Budget and plan to crush your financial goals. Remember, goals without plans are just dreams. Write down your financial goals and create your roadmap for how you plan on getting there. Change your mindset about money too. We must get comfortable talking about it, asking for it, and managing it. And when you get it, make sure to give it. Generosity goes hand-in-hand with gratitude, like I mentioned earlier. And remember, stop doing things for free that others are getting paid to do—smarten up.

1. Learn how to budget while giving yourself a bucket of money to blow. You earned it. You worked hard and deserve to enjoy the fruits of your labor.

2. Concrete plans are necessary to achieve financial goals.

3. Read about basic money management. Knowledge is power.

4. Love yourself deeply.

SPARK Notes

MONEY TEAM

Unless you have a degree in finance, most of us need a money team after we start making a certain amount of money or when our finances get complicated. I used to rely on doing everything myself, but I stopped doing that when things got more complicated. After I broke down in tears trying to do my own taxes, I never tried to do them alone again. I did not go to school to be a financial expert, but I do read about financial matters a lot because I never want to be completely in the dark when it comes to my finances. As I mentioned before, everyone should know the basics. I would rather employ an expert to assist me, not only so I do not make mistakes when things get complicated but also because someone else went to school to teach me how best to invest my money and I did not.

So, who should be on your money team? A bookkeeper, an accountant, and a financial planner. All three of these people need to be distinct and you should meet with them regularly. And how do you find your team members? Well, trust is huge and unfortunately, like in every field, there are dishonest people, so the best way to draft your team is via word-of-mouth referrals from friends or family members you trust. When you first speak with someone, make sure you vibe with them. This is your money, so you want to make sure it is in the hands of someone you trust. Ask them for two to three references and make sure you let them know you want to be involved in the money management process. I do not love the idea of handing my money over to someone and barely connecting with them. I prefer to meeting monthly or to receive a report monthly.

Also, avoid hiring your friends and family members. Personal and business should be kept separate.

Ask your trusted friends and family members for referrals to add to your money team and then vet the candidates yourself. Start with short-term contracts in case the relationship just does not work. Understand the basics of money management and hire your money team to help you achieve and exceed your financial goals.

SPARK Suggestions

1. Hire a bookkeeper to keep track of all your transactions, money going in and money going out.

2. Hire an accountant to prepare and examine your financial records and get you ready for tax season.

3. Hire a financial planner to help you create a plan to achieve your financial goals.

4. Love yourself deeply.

SPARK Notes

CHARITY

My first memory of charity comes from my dad. He is the most generous person I know. He supports so many more people than I ever knew of. His strongest advise to my siblings and I is to do good in this world without expecting anything in return and the universe will reward us for our good deeds.

I have seen estimates of anywhere from three to ten percent of your annual income recommended to be given to charity. I do not know where those numbers come from, but I do believe we all must give, because everything you give from your heart will come back to you several times over. To live a life of abundance, you must give, because that is how you get. I love giving to causes near and dear to my heart where I know exactly where my money is going and that it is reaching the people it is meant to reach. I believe charity should be private, except for in cases where a donation is made public to encourage others to match or exceed it. I always cringe when I see videos circulating on social medial of people filming themselves helping others in need. It really lacks so much tact and is embarrassing to those receiving help. Stop doing it.

I remember when I was a little girl and I would be out with my family and we would walk by a person in need in the street, my dad would make sure the whole family walked far enough past the person in need, and then he would hand me some money and tell me to run back and give it to them and that they would wait for me. I only understood why he was doing that when I got older, that he wanted charity to be given privately, without our six family members and sometimes the friends we brought along, standing around a person receiving a blessing in their most vulnerable of states. I carry that lesson with me to this day. Give always and give privately.

So, how much should you donate? I do not know. I know some religions have recommendations for percentages of annual income, but I say do what you can. Charity is not only money; there is an Arabic saying that goes something like "Every good deed is charity." Donate money, donate the clothes in your closet that have been sitting with tags on them for years, donate your school books, donate the laptop you are not using anymore, and just as important, donate your time. Whether it is mentoring youth in your community or cooking food at a shelter, give generously of your time. No one ever lost anything by giving. Imagine if we all just gave on a regular basis; everyone would have food and shelter.

Take time to purge your closet. We all have clothes hanging in our closets that still have tags on them or that we have not worn for years. Keep the (very few) items that have sentimental value, but otherwise get rid of the items you know someone else can use. Do this with your jewelry, your shoes, and your electronics. We all have things lying around the house like old phones and laptops we no longer use that can change someone else's life. I recommend donating to a place that gives your items directly to people. Better yet, if you know individuals or families in need, donate directly to them. I prefer the latter.

Dignity is also an important consideration in charity. Please make sure the items you are donating are in good condition. A torn-up and stained t-shirt you bought in Cancun belongs in the trash. Respect the souls you are aiming to help by making sure the things you are donating are clean and useable. And if you are donating directly to someone you think may need your items, you can say something like, "Hey, I was thinking about donating some of the clothes that no longer fit me, do you know of a place or person in need?" Any time I have said this to someone I know can make use of items I no longer need they have said yes. Remember, you want your charity to be private, and you never want your charity to shame or embarrass the person receiving the charity during their most vulnerable moment. Be kind and be genuine with your intentions.

I say to you: Give. Give what you can. Give to causes near and dear to your heart. Give your time and your money. Give to live abundantly. Give without expecting anything in return. Give because you are blessed, and many others are not so blessed. Give to make the world around you a better place. Give much. Give often. Give privately.

SPARK Suggestions

1. In most every case, charity should be private. Respect people in their most vulnerable moments.

2. Purge your closet of clothes and house of items you no longer need but are in good condition and donate directly to others in need. Donate to an organization that gives your items to those in need or directly donate yourself.

3. Remember that every good deed is charity. Give money. Give time. Give what you can.

4. Love yourself deeply.

SPARK Notes

SPARKPLUG IGNITER

noun

A person who creates an environment of inspired leadership and elevated growth.

Mastering each module in this roadmap will lead to career and personal development. Each of the five modules targets a different area of our overall well-being—the Health Spark, the Life Spark, the Human Spark, the Career Spark, and the Money Spark. You may need to work on all of them or just some of them. You decide. Invest in your development; it will surely pay off.

When we are in a state of contentment, when we have achieved that deep-down-inside happiness, when we become unbreakable, when we live life on our own terms, when we live fully, when we love deeply, when we create the career we have always dreamed of, when we make use of our gifts and live within our purpose, when we are generous, kind, and forgiving, when we learn to love and forgive ourselves, and when we appreciate that this crazy—and sometimes harsh—world is truly beautiful is when we become the SPARKPlug Igniter.

The SPARKPlug Igniter is a person who creates an environment of inspired leadership and elevated growth. When we are truly living, we empower those around us to do the same. Be the leader who inspires everyone around them to be the very best version of themselves. Be the leader who sets out to change the world and very well does just that.

Dear Sparkies,

If you made it to the end of the book, consider yourself a Sparkie, and I look forward to meeting you at a SPARK Live event. Thank you, from the bottom of my heart, for picking up my first book and reading it. I truly appreciate it. I hope you feel empowered to take control of your career and life. I hope you can now see that you do not have to be in a career you dread every day that does not ignite that fire in you. We all have a purpose here on earth and a gift we must share with the world.

A wonderful life is a one lived in its purpose. I wanted to write about the struggles I have had along the way in my career so far. I wanted to share the ways I overcame them and the things that have helped me grow. I wanted to share them because I know a lot of women and men in high-stress careers share similar challenges, and if I can empower even one person to get out of their comfort zone and really live, then my job here is done.

I want you to start by loving yourself, for that is the best way to receive love from others. I want you to be kind to yourself. I want you to change that internal narrative that says you are too inexperienced, you are too opinionated, or you are too much. You are here for a reason, you are an expert, and you are exactly who you are meant to be. Replace the negative voices with positive self-talk. If something sounds too mean to say to your best friend in the whole wide world, do not say it to yourself.

I want you to live fully, and I mean fully. If you hate your job, figure out how you can improve things, and if you cannot, find a new job. Go back to what that little child always dreamed of doing and ask yourself why you stopped doing it or why you never did it to begin with. Stop living your life for anyone but yourself. Keep your soul young. Write down everything you know is holding you back and you will find that the most disabling thing is fear. Crush your fear and jump into the unknown. You will never gain the highest echelons of success without taking a chance. The worst-case scenario is never as bad as you make it seem in your head.

If you never want to get married, do not. If you never want to have kids, do not do that either. Every one of us measures success in their own way so stop comparing yourself to others. The only person you should be competing with is yourself. Know that the greatest successes come after failure and that the sun is always shining behind those crazy cloudy skies. If you believe in God—I do—know that God always sees us through, even when it does not seem like he will. Remember blessings in disguise. Always look for the good in people and in every situation. The world is sweeter that way.

Be kind. Be generous. Be forgiving.

Create a morning routine for yourself. Not everyone has to start their day at 4 a.m. to be successful. I need to see solid research that backs that statistic up. Some of my super successful friends are night owls and are most creative late at night. So whatever time you do get up, create a routine that helps you clear your mind and get you energized for the day ahead. My morning Spark Hour consists of ten minutes of meditating, five minutes of journaling, and five minutes of writing down the things I am grateful for, setting my intentions for the day, and reading my affirmations, and lastly, thirty minutes of exercise. With that, I turn on some music, get in the shower and get ready for work. My favorite radio show is The Breakfast Club, but I cannot listen to it in the morning because I do not like listening to it broken-up because my work day has almost always started when it is on, so I wait to watch the whole episode later that evening or the next day in its entirety. Starting off my day in a positive way makes it more likely that the rest of my day will go smoothly. At least the parts of it I can control, which is basically my own reactions to the world around me.

If you are in a career that clips your wings, get out. If you are in a workplace where your boss is competing with you, get out. If you are at a job that makes you miserable, get out. If you are at an institution that does not recognize your greatness, get out. If you are in a relationship that you are no longer happy in, get out. Go where you are loved and valued.

Do not let the fear of failure be the reason you did not step out of your comfort zone. Success like you have never dreamed of is waiting for you on the other side of that fear.

Remember those letters you wrote while reading this book? Get them out and compare them. If you have absorbed these lessons, the second letter will be filled with much more self-love.

Be brave. Be bold. Be daring. Be fearless. Be limitless. And remember, everything you need is inside of you.

Share your magic with the world, Sparkie. It needs you. And for one last time, love yourself deeply.

Love Fore*ver,*
*Dr. Nasrie*n

ABOUT THE AUTHOR

Nasrien E. Ibrahim, MD, FACC, FAHA, FHFSA, is an internationally recognized advanced heart failure and transplant cardiologist and researcher. She has been published in top-tier journals and spoken to audiences worldwide. In addition to her medical work, she is a blogger and physician activist, but what she loves most is coaching physicians and scientists to confidently navigate their careers without compromising their dreams.

Through Dr. Nasrien's personal journey, she recognized the importance of well-being, confidence, and clarity of purpose to thrive in her career while finding joy and fulfillment in her personal life. She is a Fellow of the American College of Cardiology, the American Heart Association, and the Heart Failure Society of America. She completed her residency and fellowship at the University of Cincinnati Medical Center, followed by an advanced heart failure and transplant fellowship at the University of Colorado. She also completed her clinical research fellowship at the Massachusetts General Hospital/ Harvard Medical School.

Learn more at
www.drnasrien.com

CREATING DISTINCTIVE BOOKS
WITH INTENTIONAL RESULTS

We're a collaborative group of creative masterminds
with a mission to produce high-quality books to position
you for monumental success in the marketplace.

Our professional team of writers, editors, designers,
and marketing strategists work closely together to ensure
that every detail of your book is a clear representation
of the message in your writing.

Want to know more?
Write to us at info@publishyourgift.com
or call (888) 949-6228

Discover great books, exclusive offers, and more at
www.PublishYourGift.com

Connect with us on social media

@publishyourgift

CPSIA information can be obtained
at www.ICGtesting.com
Printed in the USA
JSHW051935020621
15462JS00005B/30